BRIEF GUIDE FOR WRITERS

Keith Drury

TRIANGLE PUBLISHING
Marion, Indiana

Brief Guide for Writers
Keith Drury

Direct correspondence and permission requests to one of the following:

Triangle Publishing
Indiana Wesleyan University
1900 W. 50th Street
Marion, Indiana 46953

Web site: www.trianglepublishing.com
E-mail: info@trianglepublishing.com

The *Chicago Manual of Style* is the preferred style guide of Triangle Publishing.

Published by Triangle Publishing
Marion, Indiana 46953

ISBN: 978-1-931283-34-2

Cover design: Jim Pardew
Graphic design: Lyn Rayn

Printed in the United States of America

Contents

PREFACE

When my essay was published in the tenth grade as a result of a national essay contest and I got a copy of the final book, I immediately fell into a romantic relationship with reading and writing. Now, after forty-five years of writing have passed, I am finally *writing about writing* in this small book.

I pray that this book will inspire many to even greater effort. Writing is hard work, but the rewards are commensurate with the labor. There are delicious treats in store for those of us who put our ideas into words so that others will be inspired to change the world. If this book only entertains you it will have failed. Its purpose is to motivate you to *commence*. A manuscript of a thousand words begins with a single sentence.

If you're a beginning writer, this book will explain the writing process and supply the hints and tips that make a writer successful. Though the book describes the process of most writers, it especially depicts the process I have honed over the years. Each writer develops their own regimen of writing, but this one will give you something to start with.

If you're already an established writer, this book will be a reminder of the process with which you are already familiar.

And, maybe it will challenge us all to practice our craft with greater excellence. I pray it may be so.

KEITH DRURY
MARCH 2008

Acknowledgements

I want to thank many of my friends and fellow writers who read the manuscript on its way to the publisher, but I should give special thanks to professional writer James Watkins for his input on this manuscript. Jim is the author of *Communicate to Change Lives* and the editor of *Writers on Writing*. His advice and suggestions significantly improved this book. Also, thanks to Dr. Jerry Pattengale for his help and to Lawrence Wilson, my editor. Thank you to my publisher, Nathan Birky, for his constant encouragement and the idea for this book in the first place.

CHAPTER ONE

THE ROMANCE OF WRITING

Like having children, the work of writing is front-loaded. The benefits last a lifetime, but the work of writing is just that—*work*. Writers put their thoughts into printed words that educate, inspire, entertain, challenge, and change the world. It's satisfying work. This little book introduces the work of researching, writing, and rewriting so that a thing of beauty might emerge—this is the romance of writing. We writers start with a cell of an idea and watch it gestate. Then we mentor our manuscript, correcting and nudging it along, and finally send off our fully-formed offspring into the world to make a difference. It's hard work, but enormously gratifying. This book aims to inspire you to stay at the task of raising your manuscript and turning it loose in the world.

IDEAS

At the core of all writing are a writer's ideas. This is obvious for nonfiction writing, but it's also true of a novel. Writing has a point of view, an idea behind the manuscript that influences readers. People go about life based on values developed from others. Some of those ideas come through face-to-face contact—a sort of social osmosis. Other ideas come from books and articles people read. Writing enables us to engage in conversation with people we have never met. Our ideas can change the way they live.

WORDS

Thinking brilliant thoughts is a worthy activity, but until we turn thoughts into words, they're difficult to communicate to others. Words are the writer's medium for communicating ideas. Words are thoughts incarnate, carriers of ideas. Writers open up a conversation with readers and invite a response. To those we meet in person, we can speak audibly. Writing ideas down makes them accessible to people we never will see. Writers are dealers in words. We're like painters only we sketch our ideas with words. When we're effective, our readers can translate our words back into ideas for pondering. Readers can rethink a writer's thoughts, and may agree or disagree, accept or adapt them. When we're successful, our words communicate ideas and our readers understand what we are trying to communicate.

> "Poetry is going on all the time inside, an underground stream. One can let down one's bucket and bring the poem up."
>
> —John Ashbery

CHANGE

Ideas have consequences. When we turn ideas into words, whole generations can be mobilized, movements begun, nations birthed, and millions of people inspired, encouraged, and built up, or even oppressed, tortured, and executed. Words are powerful.

Martin Luther's *Ninety-five Theses* sparked the Reformation. John Bunyan's *Pilgrim's Progress* inspired millions to persevere in their Christian journey. Thomas Paine's *Common Sense* helped

2

ignite the American Revolution. Harriet Beecher Stowe's *Uncle Tom's Cabin* became the death knell for American slavery. Adolph Hitler's *Mein Kampf* fueled the deaths of millions. The Bible inspires and instructs more than a billion Christians. Ideas have consequences and words are our medium for communicating our ideas. Words matter.

AESTHETICS

However, writing is not valuable just when it is useful; writing can also be *beautiful*. Writing is art. A book does not have to accomplish something to earn its keep. Beauty itself is precious. We can *enjoy* writing. Michelangelo's powerful painting on the ceiling of the Sistine Chapel does not have to protect visitors from a leaking roof or prevent the plaster from cracking to pay its way. It is worthy as an *objet d'art*. Most writers rarely rise to Sistine Chapel quality of writing, but we keep trying. When we succeed, we might have composed three or four sentences in an entire book that are simply magical. Our readers stop and reread our sentence and sigh at its beauty. If we could only write *many* such sentences! Alas, we often write with Stone Age drabness. Our prose is uninspiring and laborious. It may be true or helpful, but it's seldom beautiful. And we occasionally rise to the ceiling of the Sistine and write a sentence fit for the King. Once we've tasted a sentence of splendor we keep trying to write another one. But inevitably, we fall back to the floor in the next sentence. While writing is enormously useful, we also write for aesthetic purposes—to make a thing of beauty.

> "I revise, rewrite, edit and delete more than ever before, so much so that, ever since *Koko*, I see self-editing as crucial to the process as the initial writing."
>
> —Peter Straub

MOBILITY

Written ideas travel through time and space. Your written ideas can leap across cultural and language barriers you cannot otherwise cross. Someone in China or Chile may read your words translated into their own language.

> "I try to write every day. I do that much better over here than when I'm teaching. I always rewrite, usually fairly close-on, which is to say first draft, then put it aside for 24 hours, then more drafts."
>
> —Marilyn Hacker

A reader in Ecuador or Ethiopia may click their mouse and read your words at noon while you are still in bed in your part of the world. Written words have no geographical boundaries. They don't need an airplane ticket; they don't need a visa to travel. When you have written something worthy, a dozen people from other nations may ask permission to translate your words into their language. You'll receive thankful emails from readers in far lands, in a language you can't read. You may one day receive cheaply printed newsprint versions of your book from Asia or Africa. Or, you might get a beautifully embossed hardback edition from one of these places that becomes of greater value than the one your own publisher produced. Your heart will leap at how you have communicated ideas to people you will never meet in languages you cannot speak. Our writing can go places we never dreamed of visiting.

Even more, your writing can travel through time. Even after your body is lowered into the ground, your written words will live on. Martin Luther is still in the conversation 500 years after he was buried. We still read Thomas Aquinas 750 years after his death. The words of St. Paul influence the conversations in a million Sunday school classes every week, 2,000 years after he was beheaded. Homer died ages ago, yet we still read *The Iliad* and *The Odyssey* almost three millennia later. Words last. Even when your book goes out of print, it will still be available through an international network of online used bookstores. And all this doesn't even take electronic versions into account. A thousand years from now—if the Lord tarries—someone, somewhere in the world will use a search engine that will find your words. Those words will make a difference in his or her life.

SENSUAL PLEASURE

For the present, we still cut down trees, grind them up and print our words on physical paper. Admittedly, books are sensuous objects. We can *feel* a book. When you first get your book back from the publisher, you won't read it right away—first you'll *touch* it. You'll rub your fingers across the cover. You'll turn the pages and feel the quality of the paper, leafing through the work to drink in the attractive appearance of its typeface and layout. Even if your publisher is a lousy printer, you'll feel your book before reading it. It will bring great sensual satisfaction, like tousling the damp hair of a child after his bath. Books might someday be completely replaced by electronic text, but who gets sensual pleasure from rubbing their computer—other than Mac® users? Books are still around. There are few sensual delights for a writer that compares to the touch, smell, and sight of a quality book. Writing is a romantic work and worthy of our time.

> "I make an index of my notes and then get to the writing as soon as I can. I do a rough draft, and then I rewrite and rewrite."
>
> —Tracy Kidder

This is the romance of writing that makes the hard work worth the effort. This book introduces the writing process with the intention of encouraging writers to keep at it.

NOTES

CHAPTER TWO

INTRODUCTION TO THE WRITING PROCESS

Writing is a process, not a single task. Most people picture "writing" as typing words into a computer. Real writers know that typing is only a small task in a much larger process. Writing also includes reading, thinking, researching, note-taking, and outlining. All these happen before the typing begins. Once we have typed the first draft, the writing process continues. There are untold days of rewriting and editing to be accomplished before we send our manuscript to the editors. This chapter introduces this writing *process*. It's a long chapter because it describes a long process.

RESEARCH READING

The first step to becoming a great writer is becoming a great reader. While it's obvious that most readers never become writers, all writers start out as readers. We do three kinds of reading. First, we *read broadly* in fields different from our own. Here we find connections and examples that help us in our own writing. Second, we *read narrowly* so we're up to date in our own field and are aware of the conversation before we add our voice.

Third, we do specific *research reading* in the precise subject area where we intend to publish. We know it is impolite to speak before listening, so we don't write before we read. All of this requires us to set aside scheduled time for the disciplined "listening" of reading. A writer's schedule for completing a book project often involves a full year of reading before we type our first words into a computer. Most writers write by appointment. We block out a day or more per week (or one or more half-days) dedicated to writing. These "writing days" may actually be reading days for a year or longer. Good writing starts with good reading.

THINKING

Writers must think while reading—thinking about our own response to the conversation already occurring. While reading, we "talk back" in the margins. These notes become the basis of our future writing. We make connections and argue with writers as our own rudimentary outline begins to emerge in the margins of the books we read. When we get up from our scheduled reading time, our brains continue to work in the background as we continue to develop our thoughts.

What we read yesterday haunts our memory today as we attend a committee meeting. While others in the meeting think we're taking notes on the discussion, we're actually scribbling thoughts about our emerging book. It's slowly simmering on the back burner of our mind. Scheduling time to research dumps ingredients into our mind's slow cooker that will simmer for days. A writer's mind is always working. We are always preparing to write. Some writers put it this way, "I write twenty-four hours a day even if I only type one."

MONITORING THE MARKET

The publishing business is just that—a publishing *business.* Publishers are interested in what sells, not just what is worthy. Editors are suspicious of a work claiming excellence that no one wants to purchase. They assume the market is wise enough to determine quality. They may be wrong or right about this, but publishers who ignore the market eventually go out of business. So do writers.

Wise writers keep their eye on what is being published and where the market is headed. This means we often page through catalogs to see what's coming out. Have you ever found the title of a book you thought about writing a few years back? Most of us have. We congratulate ourselves for being on the cutting edge, and then scold ourselves for not getting around to writing the book fast enough. The best writers anticipate the market, suggesting articles or titles the publisher is already thinking about. Such writers get published.

> "To this day, I get rewrite offers where they say: 'We feel this script needs work with character, dialogue, plot, and tone,' and when you ask what's left, they say: 'Well, the typing is very good.'"
>
> —John Sayles

The market is capricious, however. A title of no interest today might be in great demand five years in the future. For this reason, writers sometimes write for inventory. We store away our work until the market comes around to us again. Writers attend writers' conferences, talk to editors, and connect with other writers in their field to discern where the market is headed. Then we submit proposals that anticipate the market. This is one of the reasons writers network with editors and attend writers' conferences—to get to know the people who take writing to market. Novice writers moan that the market does not recognize their genius. Old hands just wait for the market to shift. They know publishing is a free-market enterprise where the customer is king. Since the king decides if we get published, we pay attention to the king.

MAKING AN OUTLINE

Writers make an outline *before* we start writing. Novices often try to sit down and start typing on their first writing day. They claim, "I have an outline in my head." Veteran writers make an outline first. To avoid stream-of-consciousness manuscripts, some publishers insist writers submit their complete outline first. An outline organizes our thoughts and puts our ideas in a logical sequence. Making a good outline is half the work in writing your first draft.

CHAPTER TOPICS

The first outlining task is to turn our research notes into chapter topics. In looking over our notes, a logical sequence of chapters begins to emerge. When I make such an outline, I pile all my note cards on the floor of my writing studio. I shuffle them about, sorting and merging until a table of contents surfaces. Once satisfied, I write each chapter title on a 9 x 12 envelope and put the stack of related note cards and clippings inside the chapter envelope. Now an idea for a book has become a list of chapters. Then I drop all future notes into the proper envelope for that chapter. You can use envelopes, file folders, stacks on a table, boxes, or whatever fits your style. Finding the method that works best for you will ensure a strong table of contents outline.

SECTION TITLES

The second outlining task is making section titles for each chapter. If your publisher requires a full outline of the entire book, this step must be done early. A section title outline helps us produce a coherent full-book outline before we write any one chapter. When a publisher does not require a full outline, writers are more inclined to develop section titles as they write each individual chapter. Either way, writers rarely type a chapter without first making an outline of the section titles for that chapter.

Section titles are the bold titles of each component in a chapter. In this chapter the current section title is "Making an Outline." Outlining by section title does not always mean these titles will actually appear in the final book. They are sometimes only for the writer's reference and disappear when the text is finished. Some writers do section titling on a legal pad. Using index cards, I make this outline with bright-colored markers. I stack the cards on top of the supporting cards I already made. Then I open my word processor and type in the section titles in the order I have established with the stacks of cards on the floor. Once I have the section titles for a chapter, I am ready to take the final step of outlining—the paragraph outlines.

Paragraph Outlines

If we have more than one paragraph per section, most writers develop an outline for each paragraph before starting to type. Some writers can do this in their heads and "let the manuscript happen," but their lack of a formal outline sometimes shows in the final book. A paragraph-by-paragraph outline produces a detailed sequence to use when writing the first draft. Novice writers—and practically all students—complain, "But if I do all that, what's left to do at the writing stage?" That is precisely the point. Hard outlining makes for easy writing. Books that are carefully outlined flow smoothly from point to point. Our readers will be able to track our logical stream of thought. For this section the detailed outline—written before typing the first sentence—was:

MAKING AN OUTLINE (500 words)

Introduction paragraph:
  Outline in head not enough . . .
  Not stream of consciousness like some students . . .
  Some publishers require outlines . . .
  Purpose and value of outlining . . .

1. Make chapter topics
   Sequence and sort note cards
   Make envelopes

2. Outline section titles for chapters
   Some pubs require complete outlines of book . . .
   Explain section titles. . .
   Sometimes section titles are for writer and don't appear . . .
   Type up section titles

3. Outline supporting paragraphs
   Every paragraph needs an entry . . .
   Address objection to all this work . . .
   Show sample detailed outline . . .

4. Transition paragraph
   Like baking a cake . . . lots of sequential prep before
   popping into oven . . .

WORD BUDGET

Some publishers will expect you to include a word budget in your outline. Your budget forecasts the length of each chapter and sometimes sections. Generally, an editor will want you to keep your chapters evenly matched in length (not true of this book). Even if your publisher does not require a word budget, creating one will give you, the writer, something to aim for. We may run over or under our budget by 10 percent or so, but in general, a longer chapter will compensate for a shorter one, and the final word count will be near your budget. I keep my word budget in a spreadsheet and keep a running tally as I write, adjusting unwritten chapters down when I write a slightly longer chapter. The following was the working word budget for this book:

Words—Brief Guide for Writers

1,000	1. The Romance and Beauty of Writing
7,000	2. Introduction to the Writing Process
3,000	3. Generating Ideas
3,000	4. Rewriting Your Manuscript
2,500	5. The Writer's Lifestyle
<u>500</u>	6. Getting Started
17,000	TOTAL (before quotes and appendix)

Keep in mind that by the time you write multiple drafts, get expert input, and incorporate your editor's additions and deletions, the final manuscript may be far from your budget. But with or without a word budget, a complete outline will make reading easier. We do it as a favor to ourselves and to our readers. Beginning writers often romantically picture themselves sitting down "to type all these ideas I have swirling around in my head." Experienced writers know that if we want to end up with a good manuscript, we must first get those swirling ideas down in logical sequence by outlining. When writers say, "I took a writing day yesterday," they may not have typed a single sentence. They may have spent six hours carefully outlining thoughts so that when they do begin writing, their ideas will be sequenced so logically that the writing will flow smoothly. Outlining is part of the writing process. Baking a cake is more than taking a cake out of the oven. It also involves the sequential gathering and mixing of the ingredients. Outlining is mixing bowl work.

TYPING THE FIRST DRAFT

If we've made a careful outline, the writing will be easier and we'll be able to focus our creativity on executing the outline—especially wordsmithing. Most writers schedule a regular weekly time for writing. Sometimes we read or research during this time. At other times, we outline. By stage five we're actually doing what most folks consider writing to be—typing sentences into a computer. To write our first draft, we open the file of section titles we have already typed at the outline stage and glance through the logical sequence of ideas to refresh our mind of their flow. Then we fill it in, turning the phrases and ideas of the outline into sentences and paragraphs.

There are two ways to type the first draft: slow and perfect, or fast and messy. Some writers carefully hone each sentence as they go along, writing and rewriting each paragraph until something beautiful emerges. Others plow straight down the field never looking back. This second approach can produce a full chapter in a single day, though it will require many return trips for more cultivating. The first approach (more common among fiction writers) might only produce a page or two a day. Either method can produce a quality manuscript. It is up to you, the writer, to develop a style that fits you. Neither method is better. Both take the same amount of time by the end of the writing process. But be forewarned, writers who follow the first method are rare, and most of them are unpublished. Professional writer Jim Watkins says, "Write fast, rewrite slow." Most writers just get the first draft down and then launch the longer process of rewriting.

"Here's the secret to finishing that first book. Don't rewrite as you go."

—Laurell K. Hamilton

When this stage is completed, we have the first draft of the first chapter done! Most writers reward themselves with a steak or some chocolates when the draft of the first chapter comes off the printer. The spell is broken and we're on our way. We know there will be many more drafts in the future, but few joys can compete with the birth of the first draft of the first chapter of your first book. I print mine out, tape the pages together in one long sheet, then hang it on the wall to announce to myself, "There—I'm on my way." Then I go eat something unhealthy and delicious.

Some writers immediately begin editing their work as soon as the chapter comes off the printer. Most let it marinate for a while. Those who insist on writing a perfect first chapter before they proceed seldom proceed.

Getting an Agent

When you have a few chapters done, you face an important decision—whether or not to get an agent.

Some publishers still accept proposals and sample chapters directly from writers, but they're increasingly rare. An agent represents you to publishers, acting as your sales agent. They often have an existing relationship with publishing houses and they can get through to the acquisition editor. When an agent thinks you're ready, they pitch your work to the editor. For that service, they usually take 15 percent of your royalties and 20 percent for foreign editions. If they charge you any kind of fee, run! There have been numerous cases of unqualified and unscrupulous characters posing as agents. Make sure you thoroughly investigate their qualifications and track record in publishing.

Not only will agents pitch your work, they'll also advise you on revisions and will restrain you from submitting a work before it's ready. Good agents know which publishers are looking for the kind of manuscript you're writing. Agents will also negotiate your contract for you and can often land larger advances—and sometimes larger royalties—than you may be able to attain yourself. Most writers with an agent claim their agent's cut is worth it. An agent understands the complexities of contracts and the "boilerplate" contract is always in the house's favor.

On the other hand, if you are already an established writer with a record of healthy sales or have piqued the interest of an editor you met at a writers' conference, you may be able to contact a publisher directly. If you're really good, the publisher may come after *you*.

However, getting an agent is not as easy as getting a lawyer. Agents only take the clients they believe will be published on a regular basis—after all, that's the only way they get paid. Thus, an agent provides a checkpoint for your writing—someone who will read your work and tell you if you have a chance. Agents may suggest massive rewriting or a different approach before they put their own reputation on the line representing you. At this stage, your decision is to either sign up with an agent or go it alone. Once that is decided you can get back to the manuscript. For a first-time author, the agent will probably want to see a proposal first and then the whole book before they decide to take you on. They want to be sure you can finish the task. Agents are not interested in one-book authors. They want someone with a lot of books in their future—and a lot of commission.

WRITING AND REWRITING SEVERAL CHAPTERS

Most publishers want to see two or three sample chapters as a part of your book proposal. (We'll talk about proposals next.) Writers of nonfiction works seldom write their entire book before contacting an agent or editor. Most of us write a couple middle chapters of the book—ones that will show our best work. There are a variety of reasons why we start in the middle, but a prominent one is to avoid "clearing our throat" with a rambling introductory chapter. More than a few people who thought they had a book in them discovered that they only had a single, wordy introduction. Try selecting several middle chapters for your samples. This will allow you to target specifically a single topic and show your writing style.

> "I always use what remains of my dreams of the night before."
>
> —Eugene Ionesco

When we have two or three chapters roughed out, we return to each and improve them. All writers use their own rewrite regimen. Later in this book, I suggest a particular system of multiple drafts. You can use it, or make one of your own. But whatever you do, don't send your first draft to a publisher. Your sample chapter should show your best work. The reason the editor wants to see a few chapters is to decide if you can write. Unless you are extraordinarily gifted, you do not want to be judged on anything less than your tenth draft. At this point, your goal is to make several chapters sparkle so you can impress the editor. They're not easily impressed, so at the very least you want to prompt them to say, "You have promise."

THE PROPOSAL

If you're writing a novel, the next step is to finish your entire book. Publishers generally expect fiction writers to have a fully completed manuscript to make sure you can carry the conflict throughout the entire book. However, if your work is nonfiction you can begin to contact publishers once you have an outline and several sample chapters in hand. Publishers may want to give you input regarding your outline. They may suggest dropping several of your favorite chapters and adding others. They may offer a total reorganization of your outline or offer alternative approaches or formats. This is their prerogative and wise writers dialogue with publishers because they know the market best.

PROPOSAL

A proposal often includes a single paragraph or abstract describing your work, along with specific information on the book's target audience and a list of similar or competing works by other publishers. Some publishers have a template on their Web site describing exactly what they want in a proposal. If you have an agent, she or he will help you navigate this process. If you are your own agent, then find out what each publisher wants and follow the instructions exactly as they are stated. Some want only a proposal and if they become interested, they'll ask for several sample chapters later. Others expect sample chapters with your letter and proposal. Find out what they want and conform to it. Check Sally Stuart's *Christian Writers Market Guide,* a directory of publishers, and get the proposal format from the publisher's Web site.

REJECTION

Don't be surprised at rejection. If you get through to an editor directly, it's important to be aware that editors have hundreds (sometimes thousands) of other letters and sample chapters in the "slush pile." They may plan to produce ten new books this year. Nine might already be contracted with recognized authors who have an established customer base. You may be competing with hundreds of others to be the tenth book. Back when most publishers accepted unsolicited manuscripts, they often assigned the slush pile to an editorial assistant whose job was to return all these letters except the best five to ten. It was a depressing thought for writers, and it was a depressing job for the editorial assistant. More recently, the publishers don't even hire editorial assistants. Publishers allow agents or subcontracted editors to do the culling for them. While serving as a key executive with Zondervan Publishing, Lynn Cryderman shared with the Indiana Wesleyan University faculty that his office receives between five and six thousand unsolicited manuscripts annually. While they're all considered by subcontracted editors, few ever make it to the final editing consideration, and he could only recall one making it to the final stage.

So, be forewarned: your manuscript can be easily rejected. Agents and editorial assistants can seem capricious. They may reject manuscripts after reading only the first sentence if it bores them. They sometimes reject a manuscript because there is a misspelled word in the first paragraph. Their job is to narrow down the pile and send the survivors to the real decision makers. Your first hurdle is to survive this lower-level employee. Rejection doesn't mean your work is bad. It means that you didn't survive this time. Again, an agent can help. When agents call their friendly editor saying, "I've got a good manuscript I think you'll like," your chances improve.

If you're a serious writer, rejection will not discourage you. Few married couples found their life partner on the first date of their life. Therefore, we submit our proposal to several publishers at once. Since your proposal may languish at a publisher for six months to a year, you don't want to submit, wait, submit, and wait some more. Some publishers still pretend they are offended with multiple submissions, but if your cover letter notes you are submitting to multiple markets—and the editor wants your book—the first come, first served approach can speed up the process.

After you have submitted to multiple publishers, continue working on the current book (or the next one). The good news is that you'll be able to skip much of this painful process once you become an established writer with a reliable customer base. Your editor may come ask you, "What are you working on?" Don't give up now; every writer has to work to get his or her first book published.

One reason manuscripts are rejected is because they're submitted to houses that don't publish that kind of work. When you attend writers' conferences you will discover which publishers buy what genre, length, theological point of view, etc. You can get a quick idea of this by perusing the catalogs of these houses, but a writers' conference will provide more clarity.

In fact, across book and magazine publishing, 99 percent of all manuscripts are rejected. Most of those, however, are not appropriate for the particular house they're submitted to. If you carefully study the markets, your odds of publication can exponentially increase!

SIGNING A CONTRACT

Even if the acquisition editor likes your idea, there are still several more hoops to jump through. The editor may first have to sell the idea to a publication board made up of other editors in addition to the publisher's marketing people. Others may be pushing competing manuscripts and your editor may lose. Since most publishers print a limited number of books per year, they narrow their candidates to the best ones. Each book chosen leaves others waiting. If both your editor and executive editor want to publish your book, there are other hoops yet. A marketing committee may project your book's sales potential and predict profitability and what the break-even point will be. If you're writing a textbook, they may test the market to see who might commit to using your book in college courses. All this sounds like crass commercialism to a writer. We are sure we have something outstanding to say, but business is business. The publisher is about to invest a large sum in preparing, printing, and advertising your book before making a single penny on it. These hoops are part of the normal process.

THE CONTRACT OFFER

If a publisher decides that your book fits their publishing mission and it will sell, you can expect a contract offer. Your agent will help negotiate the contract. If you are your own agent, you'll have to do this yourself. The publisher may simply send you a boilerplate contract they use for all new writers.

Contract negotiation is beyond the scope of this brief guide, but there are matters you can address, even if you don't have an agent. The contract may specify your royalty percentage based on the wholesale price or net sales or some other amount. If your royalty is 10 percent of net, it means you will receive a royalty check equal to 10 percent of whatever profit the publisher makes on your book. If they sell one of your books for twenty dollars and make ten dollars per book, you receive a one-dollar royalty on each copy of that book. However, with deep discounts—up to 65 percent—offered to major retailers such as Wal-Mart and Amazon.com, you may not see a dime if your contract reads you don't receive royalties on books discounted more than 50 percent. Another issue is electronic rights. If your publisher owns exclusive rights to electronic as well as print, it's possible your book will never go out of print and you'll never get your rights back—as long as it's sitting on the publisher's server. Contracts also specify what is to be done with leftover books, books given away for promotion, or books tossed into a dumpster as salvage.

This is why it is so important to understand the contract—or have an agent who does.

ROYALTIES AND ADVANCES

The contract will also spell out what, if any, advance you might receive. An advance is a royalty payment that comes to you before they start selling the book. If you receive an advance of

$2,000, the publisher is "advancing" you the first $2,000 of your royalties ahead of time. This means you won't get the first $2,000 in actual royalties later —you already got it in your advance. The contract may also address subsidiary rights, foreign language rights, and a host of other issues you may know nothing about. If your book sells well you'll later discover how important these matters are. If it flops these issues won't matter much. Advances and royalty payments also have tax consequences, so your contract should be negotiated and signed with some thought. You may not need an attorney for signing on your first book, however. A veteran writer can explain the contract to you.

> "The time to begin writing an article is when you have finished it to your satisfaction. By that time you begin to clearly and logically perceive what it is you really want to say."
>
> —Mark Twain

NEGOTIATING THE CONTRACT

To be honest, new writers have limited negotiating power, so don't expect too much when starting out. Tested writers have considerably more power in negotiating contracts since the publisher takes less risk. Agents often pay their own way on contract negotiation, but you'll have to share your royalties with them. If your book becomes a classic, your grandkids may also continue sharing these royalties with your agent's grandchildren or successors too. But few of these issues matter much to a new writer negotiating his or her first contract.

For instance a publisher will often expect to have first right of refusal of your *next* book. New writers usually see this as a compliment. Publishers see it as their bread and butter since they know a first book seldom makes any money and they are hoping your next one might—then your first one will sell on the coattails of the second, more successful one. Usually new writers sign their contract quickly, go out for a celebration dinner, and then revise their schedule to provide the considerable time needed to finish the book by the established due date.

I have outlined the complicated matters of contract negotiation in a way that may imply that you need to become a shrewd negotiator to protect your work. However, I should confess that I did no such negotiation for the first book I wrote. When I got my contract I went out and bought a TRS-80 computer for $5,200 (in 1980 dollars!) and wrote the book for a $300 one-time writer's fee. I negotiated no royalties whatsoever. The book did well in its first year and the publisher cashed in handsomely. I had my $300 one-time fee.

Fortunately, this story has a happy ending. After brisk sales, the publisher offered a contract for full royalties even though there was no legal obligation. I quickly recovered the cost of my computer. The end of the story is still being written. *Holiness for Ordinary People* (Wesleyan Publishing House) is still in print more than twenty-five years later and is published in half a dozen languages around the world. It continues to pay annual royalties long after that old TRS-80 computer was paid off. While I have given advice here on negotiation of contracts, when I got my first opportunity to write a book I grabbed it without any shrewd negotiations. New writers are usually more focused on getting the book published than we are on paying off the new computer. Sometimes it works out.

FINISHING THE FIRST DRAFT OF THE BOOK

Books get finished when writers schedule time to finish them. Once the contract is signed, your appointment to write becomes obligatory. A normal writing day may start by loading the already-written complete chapter outline, then dumping out all your research cards and organizing them in concert with the outline. Then you type, fashioning sentences and paragraphs based on your outline and the supporting notes. You write, and you write. Then you write some more. Many writers motivate themselves with little rewards, promising themselves another cup of coffee or piece of chocolate when each section is done. Other writers deny themselves any food until the full first draft of the chapter is completed; that's what I do. Pick a system that results in finished drafts.

If you're faithful in keeping your writing appointments, you'll eventually have the first draft of your entire book completed. The hitch is keeping your appointments. Most writers note that two kinds of work come our way: demanding work and important work. On reflection, we know that *the demanding is seldom important, and the important is seldom demanding.* Writing is important work, but it's less demanding than most other appointments clamoring for our attention. It's easy to bump a writing appointment to the next day to do the urgent, pressing things today. But if we're undisciplined, our final deadline will arrive and we won't be finished. We'll either turn in sloppy work, or ask for an extension—both are black eyes for a writer.

Educators can be the worst offenders at this point. After a lifetime of all-nighters to finish papers in college, a last-minute value system gets deeply entrenched. Some scholars actually brag, "I work best under pressure." People like this procrastinate on purpose in order to create pressure. This approach may work for small writing assignments, but it's a slipshod way to produce a full-length book. If you work best under pressure, harness this by creating self-imposed deadlines. If we create an honest schedule for the entire project, we can then tell ourselves that "today is the last day to turn in the rough draft of chapter six." It *is* the last day if we have an honest schedule—even if we're turning the draft in to ourselves.

If that doesn't provide enough accountability, arrange for someone else to receive a copy of your work. Even the rough drafts. This works for writers—especially educators—who have something inside us that makes us want to hand in our work on time. For example, I sometimes receive just a single paragraph of work from Mike Buck, a literature professor who is crafting his first novel. Having someone to send our work to provides a sense of accomplishment. An accountability partner knows what we need—an immediate response that recognizes the work completed. A few agents—and a rare editor—will provide this immediate affirmation.

> "Writing a book is an adventure. To begin with, it is a toy and an amusement; then it becomes a mistress, and then it becomes a master, and then a tyrant. The last phase is that just as you are about to be reconciled to your servitude, you kill the monster, and fling him out to the public."
>
> —Winston Churchill

Figure out how to prod and affirm yourself along toward completing the first draft of your book. Sooner or later, if you simply schedule the time, you'll have your entire manuscript done—the first draft, that is. You should go out to dinner and celebrate—your work of composing your book is half done!

REVISING AND REWRITING

Novice writers think they are finished when the first draft is completed. Maybe that's because they handed in their first draft in the form of essays written during their school days. A first draft might work in school, but it won't work for a publisher. *The second half of writing is rewriting.* The day is gone when writers can say: "I've got all my ideas down. Now the editor can turn it into a book." (If that day ever existed to begin with.) Rewriting and correcting a manuscript is the writer's work. If you're wealthy, you can hire a rewrite editor to do this for you, but most writers do the grunt work of rewrite themselves. It's a laborious process, but when you're finished, your writing will be a pleasure to read and something a publisher might be willing to sell. An extraordinarily gifted scholar like Ken Schenck might be able to do the rewrite process in a few drafts. The rest of us need to take ten or more trips through our manuscript before it starts looking good. When we've taken our best shot, then we turn it over to the editor. (This book includes a separate chapter on the rewrite process.) At this point, we only need to remind ourselves that "90 percent of writing is rewriting." If you're a real, professional writer you may attain a third-third-third level: one-third researching, one-third writing, and one-third rewriting. If you're just starting out, the rewriting process will take more time.

SUBMITTING THE MANUSCRIPT

The second most significant day for a writer—second only to receiving a copy of our newly printed book in the mail—occurs when we send in our final draft to the editor or agent. It's like losing twenty pounds overnight. You carry this weight around with you for more than a year, and then, all at once, it disappears with a single click. This final act used to be done by typing up a clean copy of the manuscript, bundling it up in a box, and taking a trip to the local post office. Today we do it electronically. The editor's confirming email makes the writer think, *the ball is out of my court—for a while, at least.*

Actually, it can be a long while. After a year or more of breathing and eating a manuscript—and working overtime to get it sent by the deadline—we cannot understand why the editor lets it sit. Editors have other things to do. Writers learn to live with these delays. Sometimes the publisher gives us something to do during this time. We may be asked to gather recommendations for the book from prominent people. Better yet, if you are a good promoter of your book you'll want to gather endorsements *as* you write the book. It's a powerful part of your proposal. Endorsements by well-respected people in your field can be a real boost to getting a contract. And, you may need someone well-known to write your foreword. Some publishers will send out your manuscript for peer review before they even begin their editing and we may have to collate and address their input if we have not already done so in our own rewrite process. For now, we relax until we hear back from the editor. This is probably good because by now we are often weary of our own book.

MAKING CORRECTIONS

Depending on the publisher, the next step may be a total rewrite of your book by a development editor. Your manuscript may leave your desk and then spend a half year in the computer of the development editor who is assigned to your book. He or she may do a total rewrite, reorganizing, adding material, and (more often) subtracting a lot of what you said. The publisher may expect you to fight for parts that you think are nonnegotiable, but in the end, the publisher decides. This process makes a more marketable book—and we hope a better book—but be aware that the final draft you submitted may not be considered as sacred as you expect.

The next time you hear from the editor you will get another deadline. The editor will usually expect you to approve final manuscript changes—sometimes within a week to ten days. Some editors will send several editions of changes for you to approve. You can approve, reject, or revise the editor's changes. When you reject or revise their suggestions, it brings you into a discussion with the editor. Sometimes an editor will misunderstand and make incorrect changes. It's the writer's job to craft a change that will help other readers avoid that misunderstanding.

After exchanging several sets of editorial changes, you will finally receive the *galley proofs*. The galley was once a tray used for holding lead type. After the molten type was set, it was lined up in a galley tray in preparation for making impressions on paper. Next, the printer inked the galley tray and made a single impression on a clean sheet of paper. This sheet showed exactly how the final printed item would appear. This was the final opportunity for changes before the item went to press. The editor and writers saw the page with the associated pictures and page numbers and could see how all elements of the page fit together. Today the term *galley* is still used to mean the final WYSIWYG printout (What You See Is What You Get). Changes at this stage used to be very expensive and complicated. While that is not necessarily the case today, editors still expect very few changes at this stage. But, they still expect you to read and carefully check every minor detail: from the placement of quote boxes to the sequence of page numbers, as well as the accuracy of the table of contents and index. The next time you see your writing it will be too late to make changes—it will be your final printed book and it may be *years* before you can change the errors you find. Checking the galleys is not a time to *improve* your manuscript but to *correct* errors.

WAITING THROUGH THE PRINTING PROCESS

Once galleys are approved, writers get ants in their pants. We want to see the final printed copy sooner than the printing process permits. We were weary of the book when we sent it in, but now we're excited again. Soon we'll see a copy of the book we started so long ago. Some publishers will send you the first copy off the presses. Others might send your book to reviewers before you get your copy. Most publishers send out galley proofs to magazine editors about three months before the book is printed so that it gets coverage in the media, and so that reviews can appear in conjunction with the publication. No matter how your publisher handles this, you can expect to get an early copy.

The publishing and marketing machine now takes over and editors are left on the sidelines. Some publishers will send you a half-dozen or more free copies for your use. They might also permit you to purchase others at a special wholesale rate if you plan to sell the book in seminars and conferences. Some provide end-of-the-run prices if you order large quantities in advance of the first print run. When you get your copies, pass some of them on right away. Those who provided input to the manuscript along the way ought to receive an inscribed copy from you sooner rather than later. They may go out and buy a copy of their own if you wait too long. You may want to preserve your book permanently by framing it for your wall or otherwise safeguarding it for posterity. You'll also want to send a copy of your book to the person(s) you mentioned in the acknowledgments and your dedication. In a sense, this is the final office work in producing this book. Your book now is in print—it's time to sell it.

Or, at least you *hope* it's in print. It may be shocking to know that a large publisher may give you a handsome advance and take your book right down to the wire, then pull it back from printing because their plans have changed. And some publishers will publish your book and never market it—leaving it to languish on the shelves. But, let's hope your book actually gets printed and the publisher decides to put money behind it in promotion. It's time to help them!

Promotion and Advertising

Most publishers expect you to help sell your book. You probably already completed a long form, offering your time and connections to help sell the book. New writers think once they have written a book the publisher does all the rest. Wrong! Publishers often expect *you* to produce some of the sales. If you are bashful about promoting your own book, publishers might be bashful about investing in you. You might do dozens of radio or TV interviews about your book. Though the publisher will usually pick up travel costs, you should expect to do this on your own time and without pay. Radio interviews will usually be via telephone, so adjust your schedule to keep these appointments. You're also expected to promote your book when speaking at conferences. Smaller publishers will even want you to arrange to sell it. If you have your own Web site, you should also push the book there. If you're connected with a professional group, announce your book's arrival. The publisher may ask you for a list of potential reviewers, so they can send a copy to each. News releases may go to magazines and newspapers.

> "Our admiration of fine writing will always be in proportion to its real difficulty and its apparent ease."
>
> —Charles Caleb Colton

This is difficult work for modest writers, but publishers expect authors to help them sell books. We try to avoid the extremes of excessive modesty and excessive hucksterism but we are involved nonetheless. Jim Watkins explains it to wannabe writers this way: "Without ME, the MESSAGE God gave me is just SSAGE. ME is an important part of getting the MESSAGE out."

Promoting is easier once you become a veteran writer. You may still be expected to do all the above but your name may carry much of the load of selling. (This is why some book covers have the author's name more prominently displayed than the book's title.) These writers already have a loyal following. If you reach this level, you will have faithful readers who buy everything you write. You know you have become your publisher's dream writer when that happens. When the publisher knows five thousand loyal readers invariably buy whatever book you write, it provides a safety net under the publisher's risk. When this happens, you'll be a valuable asset to your publisher, and they'll start treating you as such. Until your name sells your book, however, the weight of promotion falls heavily on your shoulders.

REPRINTS AND LATER EDITIONS

As soon as you get a copy of the printed book, you'll want to touch it tenderly and read it. It'll seem fresh again. Reading your words in an actual book is thrilling. Some of your writing will seem strange—you might even admire it as if somebody else wrote it. But you won't admire all of it. Even after all the drafts and editing, you will find some errors. Most writers keep one copy of their book designated "marked copy." Here they mark all the changes they want to make in future editions. Besides errors, you will also find places where your writing is still murky. You'll be shocked at how you let these things pass; this is because we raise our standards as soon as we see our work in print. Keep any reviews of your book so you might address their critique in later editions. Because of all these things, you'll want to revise your book soon. But know that you'll have a long time to wait.

If your book sells quickly it may go into *reprint* during the first year or even within a few months. A reprint is simply another print run of the book exactly as it was first printed. If you hear about it, you will want to make the corrections and changes you have been jotting down in your marked copy. Sorry. Don't expect to make changes yet. Reprinting is considerably cheaper for the publisher than making a new edition. Most authors are stuck with the first edition through numerous reprints, often for many years, before getting the chance to make a second edition. The painful thought of books being reprinted without our changes reminds us why we should do it right the first time.

If your book continues in print for years, the editor may contact you about a *second edition*. This is your chance to get out your marked copy and revise the book. Sometimes you will drop entire chapters replacing them with new chapters. You can correct all errors and clarify sections where your prose was foggy. At this point, you will also update the entire manuscript based on newer publications and research in your field since the first edition. You'll get to update any cultural references or stories that are now outdated—the ones that younger generations now reading your book won't grasp. A second edition is a chance to release a revised and updated version of your book.

HEARING FROM READERS

Perhaps the best part of writing is *having written*—that is, having finished the task. You will be gratified when you hear from people who liked your book or use it in classes. Readers are an appreciative lot. They will thank you for your work long after you have forgotten the hard days of rewriting. Others will challenge you or argue with your points, and these are helpful too. No matter what readers say, you are always thankful that they read your book. Without readers, writers would be talking to themselves.

OUT OF PRINT STAGE

Eventually most books go out of print. Even blockbusters can go out of print in a year or two while some lesser-known books stay in print for decades. You might become one of those fortunate writers whose book outlives you—a classic of sorts. However, most books have their season, then go OP—Out of Print. You might grieve at the loss of some of your works, but for a particularly poor one, you might be relieved to see it disappear. Writers change, and sometimes they're embarrassed by their early work.

Depending on your contract, sometimes after a period of being out of print, the rights revert to you and you can self-publish the book for a smaller market. Most agents will insist on having the rights revert back to the author after six months of being out of print, but new writers often ignore this provision. Be wary of signing a contract without the provision unless you're starving and will accept a "work for hire." This is also why an agent is careful to negotiate electronic rights. A publisher can argue that if your words are online, it never actually went out of print—and you'll never get the rights back even if they're not selling a single copy over the years. If you have a family-like relationship with your publisher you may be less insistent, but professional agents usually call for reverting rights even though publishers don't like it.

In today's world, however, printed books rarely become unavailable. The Internet has connected thousands of used bookstores worldwide and most any book can be found somewhere. We receive no royalties from used sales, but it's gratifying nonetheless that people are still blessed by our book long after it goes out of print.

Publishing will change even more in the future. Your book may become available forever in electronic format. Fewer publishers today include a reverting rights clause in their contracts because your book never needs to become unavailable. Even if it's not in print, your readers might download it onto their hand-held devices. On the other hand, a printed copy might also be made available in perpetuity when your publisher sells the rights to your book to a print-on-demand publisher who will make no investment at all and will print a single copy of your book as each customer orders it. In the future people may drop by their local Wal-Mart and enter a thirteen-digit code and a small machine will spit out a single beautifully bound copy of your book in three minutes. All of these coming changes affect a writer's royalties, of course, but keeping your ideas available is still at the core of the motivation for writing. We increasingly face a future where nothing *ever* goes out of print in the sense that it becomes unavailable. This is good news for those of us who want their words to live on after we're gone.

NOTES

CHAPTER THREE

GENERATING AND STORING IDEAS

Lots of people come up with a good idea while doing mundane things like riding in a car or taking a shower. Writers get out of the shower, dry off, and write the idea down. This chapter is about generating ideas, then storing and organizing them for use in communicating to others.

WHERE DO IDEAS COME FROM?

Sometimes they seem to bubble up from the hidden recess of our id as if they have been hiding below the surface until the right time. Such ideas come from the inside. Ideas also come from the outside. We encounter them in reading and listening to others. Occasionally we can generate a new idea out of nothing by connecting invisible dots between other ideas in unrelated fields of study. On rare occasions, an idea seems to come directly from God, but writers know better than to tell an editor, "God gave me this so I hope you like it."

WRITTEN IDEAS ARE SUPERIOR TO IDEAS ONLY IN THE MIND

It seems like putting an idea on paper creates space for other ideas to come. If we hold all our ideas in our head, they churn around, seemingly blocking the entrance of other ideas. Writers put ideas on paper—even the bad ones. When we're thinking of an idea, we can't tell which are good ideas and which are bad. So we write them all down. What writer has not gotten out his or her notes of once-brilliant ideas only to see that they've lost their shine? When we think of an idea, we write it down. We can sort them later. For this reason we keep note cards available by our bedside, in our pockets or purses, and near the shower so we can preserve our most valuable resource—our ideas.

WRITING AN IDEA DOWN SEEMS TO CEMENT IT

It seems like writing an idea down on paper solidifies it somewhere into the recesses of our mind. This is why we expect students to take notes in classes—we believe writing things down helps them remember what they have heard and seen. When we write an idea down, it simultaneously goes on file in our brain. When we sort through our written notes later, we're often surprised at what we once thought was a new idea. It all seems so obvious now. This happens because, once we wrote the idea down, it became part of us and our minds cemented the idea into connection with other ideas. Now when we encounter the idea, it seems so ordinary—it has become a part of us.

IDEAS TRIGGER OTHER IDEAS

When our mind begins to generate ideas it seems like nearby areas of the brain are stimulated and join in helping to produce more ideas. Our brain seems to operate like a collaborative group having its own brainstorming session. One idea will lead to another and soon ideas come faster than we can write them. Novice writers expect this to happen while typing their manuscript—and it sometimes does. More often, though, this kind of creative ideation strikes during the normal routine of life—while driving a car, washing dishes, cutting grass. This is why we keep note cards nearby so when it does strike, we're ready to capture the flow of ideas.

> "Writing is the only thing that, when I do it, I don't feel I should be doing something else."
>
> —Gloria Steinem

EIGHT WAYS WE GET IDEAS

1. READING AND RESEARCH

Writers read to gather ideas. We read popular writing in newspapers, magazines, blogs, and books to keep in touch with the culture and the way our readers think. We read periodicals, like *Books & Culture*, that are designed to keep us aware of the trends of ideas. We read classics because we're inspired to think with these writers and generate our own ideas while reading theirs. Writers often organize reading groups to discuss with others the ideas found in a book. We're developing the habit of reading outside our field. We never know how an article or book will feed our own ideas. An editorial on immigration in the newspaper might spark an idea for writing about ancient Egyptian culture. A fiction work on Alaska could provide the exact word we needed for an article on study habits. A former student may write a phrase in his or her online blog that triggers a wonderful thought for our book.

Writers also do specific research in our own field. Until we have read all the significant works in our subject area, we have little right to join the conversation. Reading is a listening skill; writing is responding. Good communication is two way. It's rude to speak without listening first to what others are saying. This means writers often "talk back" in the margins of books and articles. This conversation in the margins becomes the fodder for our own response. Your "writing appointments" for a major writing project could mean you'll be reading for an entire year. You might say, "I'm writing today," but what you'll actually be doing is reading—attentively listening to the ongoing conversation to gather ideas.

"The story I am writing exists, written in absolutely perfect fashion, some place, in the air. All I must do is find it, and copy it."

—Jules Renard

Sometimes we agree with the ideas we're reading and will want to repeat them our own way. Sometimes we disagree and we'll construct careful arguments for our own position by reading the opposite arguments. Sometimes we'll see ideas other writers have left out and add them to the conversation when we begin writing. Sometimes our reading will set off new ideas to contribute. When we've listened to everyone else in the dialogue, we can often connect dots in a new way that nobody else has seen.

If you're writing an academic work, you will be delving into books and current journals in your discipline, scanning through databases, attending professional conferences, and signing up for e-mail discussion groups in your discipline. We don't just write a book out of our head. Books are rooted in the conversation already going on.

2. CONTEMPLATION

Ideas can be created in our mind. While many ideas come to us while hurrying to the grocery store or driving to lunch, a scheduled time for contemplation allows us to ponder and meditate to produce connections we cannot imagine when hurried. Have you ever had a dozen ideas whipping about your mind that just wouldn't come together? If so, perhaps a scheduled time for contemplation could help. Lee Haines, a retired denominational leader that I know, calls this "disciplined laziness"— purposefully setting aside time to do nothing but think. Take a leisurely walk; drive your car several hours without the radio on; sit in your backyard under a tree. Ponder your subject and seek new ideas. Step back from your frantic pace and think—this may release a flood of new ideas.

3. CONVERSATIONS AND CONVENTIONS

Minds are like charcoal: alone their heat dissipates rapidly, but piled together they heat each other up and can cook a meal. Put your single lump of charcoal with other hot coals to stimulate ideas. Many academic acquisitions editors attend conferences incognito looking for hot topics and fresh research. Conferences inform them about what's coming in the academic world. It makes sense if you are attempting to write for the academic world that you would attend these same conferences and pick up those same ideas. When you have returned from the conference, continue to hang around stimulating people. Pick thought-provoking people and go to lunch. Lift the conversation to the idea level. Test your ideas on this group. See what they say. Organize an Inklings group of thinkers like C.S. Lewis and J.R.R. Tolkien did. Bounce your ideas off them. Listen to theirs. Take notes. Watch your ideation surge. If you are serious about becoming a writer, get into one of the numerous writers' groups in your area or start one. If you're an academic writer, expand this group from idea collaboration to collaborative research and writing. Collaborate with students and other faculty members in writing a monograph or journal article to get started. Write as an understudy of an established author or recruit faculty from different universities, each writing a single chapter for a book. A book seldom comes out of a single head, and few successful writers are wolves.

4. LIVING

As writers, we train ourselves to see life through our most recent project. We're always drawing in everything and connecting it to our outline. Look for ideas on billboards as you're driving. Listen to comments in Sunday school. Seek connections to your topic while grocery shopping. While this is no substitute for scheduled contemplation, ideas sometimes appear at the strangest times. When do you get your best ideas? I get my best ideas when I'm at church. That's probably because of my subject area. Most writers have a certain place and time that seems to really trigger the flow of ideas. Since my time is at church, I often jot down ideas as if I'm taking notes on the sermon. If I don't write these ideas down, they'll highjack my mind for the rest of the morning. So I write them quickly. You probably have a certain time and place when ideas seem to bushwhack you. When would that be for you? Identify that time and place, and be prepared to tap the fresh stream of ideas for your project.

5. BRAINSTORMING

At the early stage of writing—especially before the outline—a brainstorming group can stimulate the broadening of ideas. Gather a group of creative minds and present them with a problem or issue.

A brainstorming group can take a topic, look at it from several different points of view, and produce a list of issues for you to address. The best value for such a group comes at the outline stage as you are developing the section titles. Be careful to avoid defending your own position in this group or explaining your approach; just take notes. You can discard the bad ideas later. Sometimes a group can get so productive that it's impossible to keep up in taking notes. If that happens, take along a digital recorder to capture the ideas. Brainstorming can produce a broad range of ideas for the early outline of your book—more than you can think of on your own.

> "Writing is the only profession where no one considers you ridiculous if you earn no money."
>
> —Jules Renard

6. SLEEPING

The mind of a writer should never go off duty. When you're working on a project, keep your mind constantly running like a computer does processing in the background. When we go to sleep, our mind can be trained to continue working, though in a somewhat different way. Have you ever had a great idea in the wee hours of the morning or just after rising? If so, prepare to tap this nocturnal goldmine. Great writers including John Burroughs and playwright Eugene Ionesco claimed they met characters in their dreams at night, and then filled them in the next day. Nonfiction writers solve difficult puzzles overnight so the solution can be written in tomorrow's chapter.

Night thinking is often prompted by the events and thoughts of the previous day. Reading and thinking every day on your subject can program your brain for night thinking. But be mindful of watching vivid movies or television shows before retiring because it can detract from the focus on your project. Most creative writers keep cards on the nightstand next to their bed so they can jot down ideas that have awakened them. While we can't *always* read our writing the next morning, some of the legible notes inevitably find their way into our final manuscript.

7. CULTIVATING THE "CREATIVE TRANCE"

Ideas come when we are busy and when we are purposely meditating, but they can also strike furiously when we fall into what lecturer David Poyer calls "the creative trance."[1] Have you ever gotten "in the zone" when ideas bombarded your brain like pelting hail in a summer storm? Ideas come faster than we can scribble them down. It's as if we're taking dictation from the muse. Not all writers experience this creative trance, but those who have look forward to the next time. We wish we knew how to turn it on or trigger it. I have one writer friend who seems to trigger this sort of creative energy with an overdose of caffeine. That has never worked for me.

> "Writing books is the closest men ever come to childbearing."
>
> —Norman Mailer

I have never been able to schedule it. It seems to come of its own will, but it tends to strike when I have been involved in some simple activity like cutting wood or driving my car.

It seems to follow this sequence: (1) we're doing something where our brain is barely used; (2) we're somewhat bored; (3) our minds are largely blank; (4) a single idea comes that we've thought of before; (5) a virtual flood of ideas follows in the next half hour.

If a creative trance strikes while you're driving, pull over and write as fast as you can. Scribble on note cards or scrawl ideas on a legal pad. Tear off the pages one after another and toss them on the seat. Then get back on the road. Sometimes I've chosen to drive my car for long trips instead of flying in hope of falling into such a creative trance. Alas, most of the time I just have a boring, twelve-hour drive. You can't really arrange or plan it, but once a writer experiences the creative trance, we yearn to have the experience again. It reminds us of another way the brain works—when there is little or no stimulation at all.

8. PLAY

Johann Goeth, G. K. Chesterton, George Sand, Anatole France, Lewis Carroll, the Brontë sisters, and Robert Louis Stevenson all either made puppets, designed puppet scenery, or collected toys.[2] Why are writers fascinated with childish things? Could it be that when we became adults we blocked off childish creative energies and this is a way to reconnect? We might expect writers of fiction and fantasy to be childish, but some of these writers also wrote profound nonfiction works. Maybe building a snowman, carving a wooden doll, or playing hide-and-seek releases some sort of innocent creative energy in the brain. If so, playing with your children or grandchildren might be good preparation for releasing creative energy for your writing.

Most of us have a full time internal critic on retainer. As soon as we think up an idea, our inner critic tells us the idea is foolish, impractical, or has already been thought of. "Who do you think you are?" it whispers. "That idea isn't worth writing down." Maybe adults have learned to obey this inner critic and when we play, we learn to better ignore it. Who knows? All we know is some successful writers engage in childlike play.

ORGANIZING OUR IDEAS

If we are successful at generating ideas and writing them down, all that remains is to store and organize them so we can use them later. Writing an idea down is like digging ore out of a mine.

43

The ore must still be refined and processed before we see any gleaming gold. The writer's ore is in the form of scraps of paper or index cards. Few of us are orderly enough to have all our ideas on matching 3 x 5 index cards. They may be on tithe envelopes, napkins, sales slips, or a series of printed-out emails. Our job is to store and organize them.

Writers develop personal systems for storing ideas. Here's mine: I tuck written ideas into my pants pocket after I write them. When I change my pants, I empty the pockets and toss the notes into an "idea farm." An idea farm is one of several files, boxes, or other places that are dedicated to one subject: current writing project, blogging, or future books and articles. In one case—my online Tuesday column—the farm is one wall of my writing studio. On this wall, I tape all the ideas so I can see them all at once and make connections. Periodically, I sort the ideas into piles relating to one chapter or topic, and file them into the appropriate 9 x 12 envelopes (chapters) for that project.

> "Writing is easy. All you do is stare at a blank sheet of paper until drops of blood form on your forehead."
>
> —Gene Fowler

Then I forget the notes. I treat them like seeds—and once I plant them in the idea farm, I wait until another time to harvest them. Sometimes I have an idea that turns out to be identical to one I've already written down, but had forgotten. When I return to the idea farm to harvest, I sometimes discover three different notes describing the same idea—I thought it was an original each time I wrote it. I toss out the two weaker ones, or combine all three into a new fourth note for filing in the chapter envelope. Many of these ideas become components of a chapter. A few become whole sections. Most wind up as the basis of a single paragraph or even sentence. Of course, many do not even make it into the outline—they were bland when thought of and they're bland still.

Words are the currency of a writer. Ideas are the gold reserves backing up the words. Great ideas without great words confuse our readers. Great words without great ideas behind them might only entertain. The best writers have great ideas behind what they say, and they use great words to get the ideas across to their audience.

NOTES

1. David Poyer lecture at the fifth Florida First Coast Writers' Festival, 1991, http://www.esva.net/~davidpoyer/cre.htm.

2. Ibid.

NOTES

CHAPTER FOUR

REWRITING YOUR MANUSCRIPT

Our writing seldom produces excellence—but our rewriting can, and does. Likewise, a common misconception among starting writers is thinking they can send their first draft to the publisher, and the publisher will turn it into something good. Sorry. Publishers expect writers to do their own rewriting.

Rewriting is drudgery. For this reason, many first drafts languish on hard drives unfinished. "The ideas are all there," we say, but making them into a coherent work of beauty is still unfinished. Making something beautiful is romantic, but it's time-consuming work. How do writers defeat the drudgery of rewriting? We make multiple passes through the manuscript changing our focus each time. Working through a manuscript ten or fifteen times doing a general rewrite can make us despise our work. However, if we shift our focus each time, the rewrite process can actually become a delight. Well, maybe not a delight, but at least bearable. What follows is one system of rewriting. You will likely develop your own system, but this one will help you get started. See how you might extend, adapt, and reorder these common steps in the rewrite process for yourself.

First Rough Draft: Getting Our Organized Ideas Down for Later Improvement

After the research and outlining, the first draft might feel like a final product. To become a writer of excellence, however, we must discipline ourselves into treating the first rough draft as just that—a *rough* draft. This is why most writers put their draft away for a while and move on to other chapters—it's too discouraging to hang around very long with a rough draft.

Some writers, especially fiction writers, labor for hours over each paragraph. For them the rough draft may indeed be closer to completion. Nonfiction writers often type straight through the first draft based on their outline without looking back. After they finish, they know there's still a lot of work to do before the manuscript "sings." Therefore, we save the first draft in several places and save it in our other email addresses in case a tornado blows our office away. Then we move on to the next chapter. Many writers do not even correct spelling or grammar as they type the first draft. Slowing down to do so can diminish creative energy and slow down the process. When these plow-down-the-furrow writers think of a quote that is not in their notes they insert a statement like this: <*insert James Michener quote here*>. We know we will be passing this way again and will look up the quote on a second pass. Thus, we move on before we get

> "Writing an informative yet compact thriller is a lot like making maple sugar candy. You have to tap hundreds of trees . . . boil vats and vats of raw sap . . . evaporate the water . . . and keep boiling until you've distilled a tiny nugget that encapsulates the essence."
>
> —Dan Brown

too bogged down on the first draft. We'll revisit it in a few days or a week.

This is not to say we are allowed to be sloppy writers. We research carefully, quoting verifiable sources so we can avoid saying "A story has been told," or "Some say . . ." Those of us in the academic community must learn to generate new ideas and new thinking instead of simply stringing together pages of quotes from other sources. Writing a textbook is more than doing a literature review. Our dialogue must be crisp and lively and presented in such a way that it captures a reader's interest and brings them into the dialogue. If we're doing academic publishing we need to keep the sources of our quotes and references so we can accurately document them. The first draft may be messy, but that's not because we're messy writers. Even our best work is messy compared to a high standard of excellence.

Second Draft: Cleaning Up and Correcting the First Draft

After a week or so, we return to the first rough draft to correct errors and clean up the mess we made. This time we look up our inserts and rewrite garbled sentences. The second draft is laborious, requiring minor creativity but major time. We load the first draft and grind through the manuscript page by page. Some writers even do this sort of editing with a football game running in the background or while waiting at the doctor's office. It's just plain hard labor to clean up the manuscript.

THIRD DRAFT: FURTHER REFINING THE MANUSCRIPT

After letting the manuscript marinate another week or two we are ready to take a third trip through for further refining. Sections that seemed lucid a few weeks ago will now seem garbled. We work at crafting sentences to make our thoughts clear, and we eliminate repetitive sentences. When the logical flow seems jumbled, we move paragraphs around or sometimes add new ones. Sometimes we substitute whole paragraphs or insert new examples we have thought of since the first draft. When finished with the third draft, we're usually willing to show it to a few close associates. We're still working on other chapters but now we have *this* chapter cleaned up enough to share it with a second set of eyes. But it's far from ready to send to a publisher.

FOURTH DRAFT: INCORPORATING RESPONSES FROM OTHERS

Few practices improve a manuscript more than incorporating the expert input from others who read the third draft. Whom would you recruit to read and input your manuscript? If you're dealing with theological issues, which theologian could help? Should you run your manuscript past a business professional, pastor, student, someone who never went to college, a missionary, biologist, or other professional in your field? Who can read your work and be bold enough to "talk back to you"?

Some writers get two or three readers. Others recruit as many as ten readers at this stage, depending on the nature of the work. It's time consuming to input a manuscript and sometimes you'll need to barter to get this help. For example, offer to read their work later if they agree to read your manuscript now. Usually this sort of input comes back to us on paper. We print out multiple copies of a chapter and ask for their response in a week or at the latest, two. Seldom does a faithful reader need more than a week to read and critique a single chapter. By giving them our work one chapter at a time, we're asking for less commitment. They'll be quicker to respond.

> "The art of writing is the art of discovering what you believe."
>
> —Gustave Flaubert

When you get all (or most) of the responses returned, you can lay out all matching pages and decide how the manuscript needs to be changed. If several readers say on the margin of page 7, "I don't get this" or "Huh?" you know you have some rewriting to do. These experts may also challenge your facts, or they might suggest additional insights you left out. They might call for you to dial down any hyperbole or they might scoff at cultural references like, "Where's the beef?"—stuff that younger people won't get. The reader input draft is painful and can make you feel like giving up on your project altogether, but if you can stand the heat your manuscript will be that much stronger. Besides, when do you want to hear these comments—privately when you can correct them, or in critiques after you have published the book? As painful as this part of the rewrite process may be, it's worth the hit on our egos to advance the manuscript.

In this draft, you still work with a single chapter and often do it at a time other than your regular writing appointment. When all chapters have been through the reader input draft, you're ready to work with the entire book manuscript as one piece (which you get to do from now on).

FIFTH DRAFT:
DELETING AND CONDENSING DRAFT

By now, you may be tired of your book. You've written the first draft, then edited each chapter several more times. You're probably weary of messing with it. You'll have a powerful urge to send it off "as is"—or toss it in the wastebasket and forget the whole idea. You may say to yourself, "What more can I do?" There is more, even though you'll groan at the notion of slogging through the whole manuscript again. The trick to improving your manuscript from now to the end is to do "specialty editing"— revising the book while doing one kind of editing each trip through.

On the first specialty edit, find things to delete and condense. When you read the entire book in a single reading, unnecessary sections will glare back at you and you can delete them. You'll spy rabbit trails that are not germane and you can eliminate them. We writers hate to delete whole paragraphs we have already honed several times, but we must. The truth is, however, most of us don't discard them. We paste them at the end of the manuscript as we go, then paste the entire collection into a new document pretending we'll use them later in another book— occasionally we actually do. When we read the entire manuscript at one sitting, we're impatient to get through it. This makes us more like a real reader. Therefore, we sometimes restate whole paragraphs in a single sentence and whole pages become just a paragraph. The resulting manuscript is tighter or more economical rather than the verbose and wordy draft it was when we started this rewrite stage.

SIXTH DRAFT:
SEARCHING FOR AND INSERTING
RELEVANT QUOTATIONS

I'm not referring here to footnotes or longer academic quotations; you already included those in the first few drafts. This pass is for finding and inserting quips and quotations that communicate your message with the clarity and brevity of a bumper sticker. It's a fun pass through the manuscript. Most publishers expect you to cite every source, so make a photocopy of each quote and the masthead of the periodical or copyright page from the book. (They will often ask for these copies.)

Besides the quotations you collected in your research, you might also research your topic online at *worldofquotes.com, brainyquote.com* or at one of the dozen other online quote collections. Writers once used *Bartlett's Familiar Quotations* for this sort of work, but now most of us research quotations online. Remember that it's your job as the writer to attribute quotations accurately. All too often we find identical quotations attributed to Winston Churchill, Oscar Wilde, Benjamin Franklin, and John Maxwell. Each of these may have said it, but your job is to find out if he or she really said it, and who said it first. Sometimes these quotations fit nicely into an existing paragraph. At other times, the publisher may want quotations to sprinkle here and there throughout the book. In this latter case, you will put the quotations at the end of each chapter with a note, and then the designer will place

> "Writing a novel is like making love, but it's also like having a tooth pulled. Pleasure and pain. Sometimes it's like making love while having a tooth pulled."
>
> —Dean Koontz

them on the proper page. Some writers hire research assistants to do this work, but remember if you delegate this to others, the writer is the one ultimately responsible for the quotations being accurate.

SEVENTH DRAFT:
FINDING WEAK WORDS AND
SUBSTITUTING BETTER ONES

This edit is done in either one or two steps. The one-step method does this electronically, finding the weak word and replacing it with a better word as a single step. The two-step method starts by reading a printed manuscript, marking the weak words: passive verbs (has, was, is) and bland nouns. (The traditional marking is "bw." It's placed beside a word that needs to be replaced with a "better word.") The writer returns to find a better word in the second step.

On occasion, your word processor's thesaurus can be utilized at this stage, but such a method should be employed with prudence for it will recurrently assemble your sentences in a mode out of character with your individual technique—as this sentence just illustrated. If you're a good reader and have an adequate vocabulary, it's usually best to think of the better word yourself. This is an easy trip through the manuscript and can be done while riding in the car or even sprawled out on a beach. After you finish this trip through the manuscript, it will have the *best* words in every case and the manuscript will have retained your own style. This is when your manuscript will begin to shine. (You can do this and the following five drafts in any order.)

Continuity Draft:
Finding Repetition and Bringing Continuity to the Whole

This is an edit of connections. We read the entire manuscript, searching for connections to make and repetitions to remedy. We turn the book into a coordinated whole. At this stage, you may refer to other parts of the book where you cover an idea in greater detail. You might slim down the first mention of an idea so you don't steal the thunder from later more complete coverage. Not all repetition is bad—sometimes we purposefully repeat an idea to make a point (as this book often mentions the concept of "writing by appointment" because of its role in the epilogue). Some writers—and practically *all* fiction writers—plant allusions early that will later fit into the unfolding story. Others insert stealth comments that dawn on the reader later in the book. When this edit is finished, your book will be a single harmonized whole.

> "Hard writing makes easy reading."
>
> —Wallace Stegner

Reading Level Draft:
Varying Sentence Length and Breaking Up Long Sentences

Even if you have carefully constructed your sentences using the finest grammar, it's still possible you might end up with a manuscript that's too difficult to read because you have written ponderous sentences with too many words and phrases in them, making the reader miss your point in the process of reading too many words. (The previous sentence had 57 words and rates 22.8

on the Flesch reading scale and 12.0 on the Flesch-Kincade grade level.) Saint Paul got away with 57-word sentences. You won't. In Microsoft Word, check the reading level by running the spelling and grammar check combined. Set this in MSWord Tools/Options. It produces a report at the end of the check. Writing at the twelfth-grade reading level does not necessarily indicate that you're a deep writer; it may simply mean you are obtuse. Most of us want to keep the attention of an average college student who functions at the eighth- or ninth-grade reading level. In this edit, break up long sentences, add surprising little sentences, and substitute shorter words for longer ones. When you're finished, you'll have a book providing variety, spice, and ease in reading. The monotone length of sentences will be gone. It works. (The sentences since "Saint Paul" in the preceding paragraph rates 64 on ease and 7.7 grade level.) Revising your manuscript opens up your writing to a larger readership.

READ-ALOUD DRAFT:
FINDING AND FIXING SENTENCES
WHERE READERS MIGHT STUMBLE

Have you ever stumbled while reading and had to go back and reread a sentence to get it more clearly? You can find these in your own book by printing off the manuscript and reading it out loud as fast as you can, circling each place you stumble. Since *you* wrote the book, you'll need to read it fast to mimic a reader's first encounter with your words. After the entire manuscript is marked, return to the electronic version asking why this sentence caused you (the *author!*) to stumble on your own words. Usually all we need to do is change the word placement or eliminate similar words in a sentence. Some can do this while reading the electronic version but most of us like to do this with a printed copy. It's an easy repair job that trains us while we're making the corrections. When finished, our prose begins to flow as smoothly as the lyrics of a song.

Underliners Draft: Finding and Honing the Best Lines on Each Page

When readers consume your book, you expect them to find wonderful phrases to underline. This trip through the manuscript attempts to influence which phrases they underline. We read the manuscript looking for our best quotations and most succinct phrases. When we find these sentences, we rework them into something memorable—a quotable phrase. If a reader is going to underline your book, why not pick what they underline? (The previous sentence was my underliner for this page). What a delight to pick up a copy of your book ten years after you wrote it and discover that readers underlined precisely the phrases you intended. It's language geo-caching. It's true that an increasing number of publishers insist on pulling out all these underliners and placing them in boxes to help readers find them. Nevertheless, finding and reworking the best quotable lines in your book is fun, even if they wind up in a pull-out box. If you craft these underliners right they may appear in other books in the future. Do this draft and your book will begin to become art.

> "Writing is manual labor of the mind: a job, like laying pipe."
>
> —John Gregory Dunne

FIRST-LINE-OF-PARAGRAPHS DRAFT: WRITING A CRISP FIRST LINE FOR EVERY PARAGRAPH

The first line of a paragraph is like a headline—telling the whole story in summary. Novice writers tend to use their first line to set up later sentences, unfolding their logic in Germanic style so the punch line can pop out at the end. Most American readers expect you to "start at the end," announcing your main idea and then expanding on it in the rest of the paragraph. If you're willing to adapt to the American reading style, this edit takes you back through your entire manuscript to write a new first sentence that will frame the entire paragraph. Your editor might insist on it and your readers will appreciate it. Sometimes we simply revise the first sentence of each paragraph already in the manuscript, but more often we have to write a new first sentence, then rework the previous first sentence to become the second. It's a fun edit and a great gift to your readers.

> "I can write better than anybody who can write faster, and I can write faster than anybody who can write better."
>
> —A. J. Liebling

ENGLISH-GRAMMAR DRAFT: CORRECTING ENGLISH-GRAMMAR ERRORS

Some writers do this edit earlier, but if you've done a lot of rewriting—and you should have—it's better to do this at a later stage to catch any mistakes added in your rewriting. You may have caught and corrected numerous grammar errors in earlier passes, and yet errors still exist. You just can't see them. The manuscript may need another set of eyes. Some writers barter with other writers or a grammarian to get this edit done, promising to provide the service for them later. Even after two sets of eyes have done the work, your editor will still find dozens of fixes that slipped by everyone. When this trip is finished, your manuscript should be as clean as you can make it.

Tender Sanding And Polishing Draft

You're almost done! You now have a manuscript that is clean, clear, lyrical, and quotable. After letting the book sit a few days, take another trip through and lovingly adjust a few things here and there. This is a satisfying edit. By now, you are beginning to be proud of the work again. This time through, adjust and fiddle with sentences until you can't see anything else that can possibly be changed. (But don't worry because your editor will still find changes for you!) When you walk away from this draft, the finish line will be in sight. You might even start thinking about writing your next book.

Finishing Check

If your writing schedule is on track, you'll have one more day for a final read before sending the manuscript to the publisher. This edit is like the final check a bridesmaid gives to the bride before she walks down the aisle. It does not require great energy. Some writers do this final read pretending they're reading the printed book as a reader instead of the writer. There may be a few hairs out of place, a collar to straighten, and a wrinkle here and there to smooth out, but mostly you will just enjoy reading your work. This last trip through gives you the confidence to honestly write the cover note to the editor, "I think you'll like this manuscript." You know you gave it your best shot. You're now ready to send it off to the editor as you would send your daughter down the aisle. Send the email and head out for a celebratory dinner!

CHAPTER FIVE

THE WRITER'S LIFESTYLE

Writing is not just an activity; it's a lifestyle. It's more than something we do on the side even when we do it on the side. A writer's approach to living is what produces written works. This chapter is about that lifestyle.

SELF-IMAGE

If you are writing, then begin thinking of yourself as a writer. Quit saying, "I plan to *become* a writer" or "*Some day* I will be a writer." What you mean is that you intend to get published someday. You don't have to get published to be a writer; you simply have to write. Begin writing and consider yourself a writer from then on. This will establish a mental attitude that will help you set time to write. Writers write. Writer wannabes let other demands crowd out their writing time.

HANGING AROUND WITH OTHER WRITERS

If you're not attending writers' conferences, sign up for one. There are numerous conferences each year with modest registration fees and helpful seminars. You brush shoulders with other writers and make vital face-to-face connections with the editors who might some day buy your manuscript. Consider attending the writers' conference of your academic discipline or one of the many Christian writers' conferences such as at Mount Hermon, California, Sandy Cove, Maryland, or The Wesleyan Publishing House's conference in Indianapolis. There are others, but these are especially good with many editors to whom you can show your proposal. Get on the mailing list of writers' conferences so you can move around each year and connect with a different crowd. This will help you see yourself as a writer. It also provides inside tips and hints on the market. You will likely meet other writers who live near you and you can set up your own Inklings group to spur one another along and to provide accountability.

Jim Watkins tells authors there are three secrets to getting published: network, network, and network.

PRACTICING

Writing is like playing the violin—we improve by practice. The writing lifestyle prompts us to write regularly, often 500–1,000 words a day, even though others will never see most of them. Novice musicians sometimes imagine themselves giving a concert in a huge hall packed with an applauding audience. Novice writers sometimes have a similar dream— producing a widely acclaimed book. Yet the writer cannot expect an acclaimed book without practice any more than the violinist can expect a standing ovation without practice. The next few sections give some ideas about writing *for writing's sake*, and practicing on smaller groups before launching your major book.

WRITING ARTICLES

This book is mostly about writing books, but if you're a writer, don't overlook the rich field of article writing. Writers need readers, not just a book in print. It is true that books bring greater respect, but if you want readers and not just respect, consider writing for periodicals. If you publish a book with a smaller publishing house they may consider it a best seller if it sells 20,000 copies. Bigger houses won't use that term until 100,000 copies are sold, and there are only 500 of such best sellers out of the 1.2 million books tracked by Nielsen Bookscan. If you're writing a scholarly work, sales of 500 may be considered best-selling. According to *Publisher's Weekly*, of the 1.2 million books tracked by Nielsen Bookscan (2004 data), many books in print have a very small circulation:

> "Writing became such a process of discovery that I couldn't wait to get to work in the morning: I wanted to know what I was going to say."
>
> —Sharon O'Brien

Sales of 1.2 million books in print
950,000 books sell less than 99 copies
200,000 books sell less than 1,000 copies
25,000 books sell more than 5,000 copies
500 books sell more than 100,000 copies
10 books sell more than 1,000,000 copies

And here's the most amazing statistic of all: the *average* book sold only 500 copies. If readers and influence is your desire, consider periodicals. One article in *Decision* will reach over two *million* readers. So if you're a writer, at least consider periodicals and don't hold all your good ideas for a later book.

WRITING FOR YOURSELF

We start by writing by and for ourselves. We write private journals and articles we "publish" on our own hard drives long before we expect an audience to pay for our public work. We open these files and edit and polish them until they're beautiful. Then we save them again, satisfied that we're getting better at writing. We don't consider private writing a waste of time if we're improving. Practice writing helps us improve, or at least keeps us from losing our touch. If we are a mediocre writer, we can become a fair writer by practice. If we are a fair writer, we might become good. If we are good, we might even become excellent. All this comes in the practice room, not at concert performances. Writers write—even when we are our own audience. Of course, we are never the only reader. God sees everything we do. Besides ourselves, we know we can always count on one Reader.

WRITING FOR INVENTORY

All practice writing goes into "inventory." The old artist's adage is also true for writers: "You've got to fill your attic before you fill your pockets." Artists produce art because they are artists. If nobody buys the artist's first painting, the artist shouldn't whine about being unrecognized. He or she should just keep painting. Artists fill their attic with the confidence that some day their style might take off and they'll be able to bring down those old pieces and sell them.

Writers develop complicated filing systems on our hard drives and carefully file our practice writing knowing that some day *some* of this work will be marketable. Once you become an established writer, your editor might ask you to write a piece exactly along the lines of an old item you wrote twenty years before. You can load the file, polish it up, and in a single week submit a manuscript that perfectly meets the editor's needs. It happens!

Rejected pieces also go into inventory. James Michener's editors rejected an entire chapter of his book *Texas.* It described the conflict between Sam Houston and Santa Anna. The rejected chapter came out of the book and went into his inventory. It was later published as the novella *The Eagle and the Raven.* Likewise, the editors rejected Michener's chapter on the courageous journey of five Brits that was originally part of his book *Alaska.* It too went into his inventory and later emerged as the short historical novel *Journey.* Both of these shorter works are wonderful pieces. The editor was right— they did not belong in the longer work. But their rejection enabled two other works to be born. The writer's inventory is not a morgue but a savings account. If publishers aren't buying your work, keep writing and storing it all in inventory.

> "Vigorous writing is concise. A sentence should contain no unnecessary words, a paragraph no unnecessary sentences, for the same reason that a drawing should have no unnecessary lines and a machine no unnecessary parts."
>
> —William Strunk, Jr.

START WITH YOUR CURRENT AUDIENCE

Few writers are satisfied with a readership of one or two, even if God is the second reader. We want others to read our ideas and become inspired, informed, and entertained. This does not mean, however, that we have to sell 5,000 books. We start by writing to our current audience first. If you write a full-length book who would read it? Who do you *know* would read it? Your mother? Your children? Your colleagues? Students?

Church friends? Fellow biology professors? This is your current audience; start by writing for them. Send these people a short article and invite their comments. Start an online academic journal or public blog, inviting people to respond. Self-publish a short work and give it away free. Test your own marketability with your current following. See how your work gets received and how it spreads word-of-mouth.

Writers sometimes imagine a publisher can make our book successful by advertising. Though there is a bit of truth to this, the publishing business has hundreds of stories of major books that flopped after a huge investment in promotion. Instead, write a weekly blog and watch the traffic. If we cannot get a hundred people a day to read our writing for free, how can we expect them to pay for our book? On the other hand, if you publish your writing (even practice writing) on the Internet and a thousand people come to read it every week, publishers will take notice. You will have a following and some of your readers will actually pay for your writing. Writers don't wait until they get published on paper to spread their words. They start with their current audience.

> "Now the writing in the head, I definitely do every day, thinking about how I want to phrase something or how I'd like to rephrase something I've already written."
>
> —Stanley Crouch

PREPARING MENTALLY

Writers are superstitious folk. We psych ourselves up for a writing day like a football fanatic would on game day. We're careful of what we eat the night before so we get a sound sleep and aren't groggy. We're careful of what we watch on TV the night before we write. We read something on our subject before going to bed. We fall asleep with thoughts of our project on our mind so our brains will be in gear as we sleep. We follow a strict routine on our writing day. Some writers cook a large protein-rich breakfast of eggs and bacon before writing. Others, including myself, deny themselves any food until they have written at least 1,000 words—the breakfast is a reward. Writers often have a "writing uniform" like a cherished wool sweater or flannel shirt (in my case, an old corduroy jacket) which is donned to announce to themselves the nature of the day's work. I always polish my shoes before writing just to signal to myself that I am meeting the largest audience I will ever address—my readers. Whatever it may be, most writers develop some sort of personal routine that prepares our minds to write today.

FIND A PLACE

Most writers have a special place for writing. I've written in the living room with a laptop perched on a pillow, in a study carrel at the library, in my home office, and at a hideaway cabin in the woods. Some places are particularly suited to writing. You may prefer writing amidst messy piles of clippings and stacks of old manuscripts. Or you might prefer writing by a window where you can gaze out across a lake to gain inspiration. Maybe your kitchen table inspires you most. Many writers dream for a dedicated place we can consider our own writing studio. This is a place where no one else is allowed, a private womb-like environment where we snuggle to write and nothing else. Few of us can afford such a space until we've published half a dozen books, but we can still dream about it until it becomes reality. Professional writers like Jim Watkins insist on *one* place in which to write. They believe our brain begins to associate writing with that spot. You sit down and the brain says, "start writing!" This place can be a powerful association trigger for writing! (Jim always writes at a desk that he built with his father when Jim was in high school. Needless to say he has a long association with that place.)

"If there is a knack, I don't really have it. Talent— I really don't know what it is anymore. But I have perseverance, and I think that's more important. I do have the ability to sit in one place for a long time and not get bored. This is a good thing for a writer. Because everything I do starts out a mess. You'd be embarrassed to have anybody look at it. And you just have to sit with it and push it around— and throw half of it out, and take the other half and mush that around a little bit. It just takes time. Most people give up."

—Garrison Keillor

Whatever place you select, the chief aim is to remove distractions. Turn off your phone and close the email. Distracting pictures and to-do lists should be removed. When we pause to think of a better word, the tiniest distraction will get us off track. Writers often have odd obsessions about their equipment as well. For John Steinbeck it was sharpening pencils and finding the exact brand of pencil that worked best for his hand-written manuscripts. Writers sometimes insist on using the same typeface and font size on their computer screens no matter what they have to do to change it before sending it in. All this reminds us of how easily we are distracted. Writing is hard work, and there are always a multitude of sirens to lure us off course.

You might develop other idiosyncrasies in your writing regimen. In order to stay true to my target audience I often tape a picture of one or two real people on my computer when writing. Glancing at this real person helps me eliminate gobbledygook from my writing. I write a sentence, punch the period, then look up to see their gazing face. If I determine that what I've written won't make sense to the faces in these pictures, I rewrite it. They keep me honest and bring continuity to my "voice."

But, if I put up the wrong picture, I miscalculate the audience and the manuscript becomes a flop. (We'll see if I picked the right person for this one.)

COMMENCING

The hardest part of writing is starting. Even the great pros have trouble here. The bigger the writing task the slower we are to begin. My computer desktop needs to be cleaned up. The carpet needs to be vacuumed. I should really check my email first. There's something funny about the casters on this chair—maybe I should turn it upside down and check them out. Did I leave dishes in the sink? I wonder why last week's Amazon order isn't here yet? Gee, the grass needs to be cut; maybe some fresh air will clear my mind. These and a dozen other thoughts conspire to keep us from commencing.

Writing the first paragraph is frightening. Editor Alan Miller helped me overcome this fear twenty-five years ago when we were serving as reporters at a general conference. He quipped, "Anyone can write the bottom of a story; it's the top that takes talent—write the top last." Ever since I heard him say this, I've started every article or chapter by typing the word "TOP" in capital letters repeatedly for a full paragraph. Then I begin writing the *second* paragraph. I return later to write the top last.

> "Writing the last page of the first draft is the most enjoyable moment in writing. It's one of the most enjoyable moments in life, period."
>
> —Nicholas Sparks

John Steinbeck started his writing days for several of his books by writing a letter to his editor first thing every morning—a letter he never sent. He described the progress of the manuscript, how he was feeling that day, rambled on about his personal and family life, discussed the state of his pencils, then turned to work on the real manuscript. Two sets of these letters were preserved and are now published under the title *Journal of a Novel (East of Eden)* and *Working Days (Grapes of Wrath)*. His daily preamble letter broke the spell of morning writer's block. In these letters he could "clear his throat" for the serious writing ahead of him. Whatever system you develop for getting started, the dragon of delay must be slain. Writers who get published commence.

REWARDING PROGRESS

Maybe it's too juvenile for you, but some writers set up elaborate systems of rewarding themselves for writing. Writing is the epitome of delayed gratification. We research for a year, write the second year and wait another year for the editor and publisher to get the book into print. If we're writing a major book, what we type today may not appear in print for years. For these reasons, we invent a more immediate reward system. As you practice the writer's lifestyle, you will uncover what motivates you in the short term. For my wife, it is definitely chocolate. For me, it's a giant breakfast of ham, eggs, and fried potatoes after I've written 1,000 words. When a manuscript hits various milestones, I head out for a steak. As a numerical prod, I update a spreadsheet tally of words written so far and send it to several partners daily to show my progress by the end of a day. These little rewards keep us going until we reap the greater rewards later on.

> "Talent is helpful in writing, but guts are absolutely necessary."
>
> —Jessamyn West

Ok, I finished this section—I'm going to go cook breakfast!

Epilogue

If you're still reading this short book, you must be a writer. You wouldn't have come this far if you were satisfied with reading about writing more than actually writing. So, when will you commence?

Delay is our enemy. We say, "I'll get to my writing as soon as my schedule lightens." It never does. We tell ourselves, "When summer comes, I'll start writing again." But when summer arrives, so does the grass. And then there are vacations to be taken, things to be repaired, and, before you know it, the leaves start to fall and need to be raked. The months have passed and not a word of writing was done. Some folks say, "I plan to write when I retire." But we know that few retired writers can get published if they haven't developed a following while still actively engaged in their field. Some say, "I'm waiting for inspiration," not recognizing that writing comes more by perspiration than inspiration. There are a dozen other reasons to delay and only one to begin: *beginning is the only way to finish.*

Setting Your "Appointment to Write"

We find a writer by looking at the person's schedule. Writers schedule time to write. This is the writing appointment so often mentioned in this book. It's the single most important discipline for the writer. Writers make an appointment to write and then guard it scrupulously. We treat it like any other appointment. We refuse to let other demands cause us to treat writing as if it's free time. We know writing is hard work and it deserves an important spot on our schedule. So when will you make your next appointment to write? On which day? At what time? For how long? Where will you meet your manuscript? Schedule the times you will read, research, outline, and write.

Once you've firmly established a sacred appointment, the river of work will flow. Some of your former activities will simply vanish. You'll find that you become more efficient at other activities and that some of them can just wait. People who would have come to you with questions will get their answers from someone else. You'll watch less TV. Your writing appointment need not hamper your effectiveness at your day job—it might even increase your efficiency.

The biggest difference between writer wannabes and actual writers is that *writers write*. It's that simple. Setting a time is the first step in this journey of a thousand miles. So what about next week? What time will you set aside to *commence*?

Sample Style Guide

The following is a sample of a publisher's style guide, and is typical of the style used for book publishing. Check with your publisher to find out what style it uses.

Author Guidelines

I. Creating Your Work
    A. General Instructions
    B. Formatting Your Manuscript
II. Documentation
    A. Documentation Requirements
    B. Standard Method
    C. Author-Date Method
III. Permissions
    A. Using Copyrighted Materials
    B. How to Seek Permission
IV. Submitting Your Manuscript

I. Creating Your Work

A. General Instructions

1. Meet the word count listed in your contract. Since the page count and price of your book will be determined before you submit the final manuscript, it is very

important to meet this word count. Do not vary the word count by more than 2,000 words without permission from your editor.

2. Authors are required to obtain permission (and pay any fees) for the use of copyrighted material in their work. See the section on permissions for more details.

3. Cite research findings and other authorities *only* when they clearly aid in understanding the text. Do not cite simply to add material or to give the appearance of thoroughness.

4. Cite opinions only when they significantly enhance your view or represent a major stream of contrary thought and are well documented by an authority in the discipline.

5. Use only well-documented facts, quotations, or other illustrative material. *Never* introduce material with phrases like "The story is told" or "It has been said."

6. Use straightforward declarative sentences. Avoid overuse of the passive voice.

7. Make words pull their weight. Avoid constructions that add words but not meaning. Example: "As we closely examine the first chapter of this beloved epistle, we will immediately notice three things." Better: "Paul makes three points in this chapter."

8. Do not cite current events which quickly become dated. (References to 9/11, for example, are already passé.) Do not use dates to describe events unless the date itself is meaningful.

9. Do not use academic abbreviations that may be unfamiliar to students.

10. Use italics sparingly for emphasis. Use exclamation points sparingly. Use quotation marks sparingly.

11. Do not use boldface for emphasis. Do not underline.

12. Add subheads to organize your work and aid readers in navigating long blocks of material. See examples in the Formatting Your Manuscript section.

B. FORMATTING YOUR MANUSCRIPT

1. *The Chicago Manual of Style*, 15th edition, is the standard style book for many publishers. Follow this style except where contradicted by the house style sheet from the publisher.

2. Manuscripts not properly formatted will be returned for revision.
   a. Page Size: 8 ½ by 11 inches.
   b. Margins: 1 inch, all margins.
   c. Font: Times New Roman 12 for *everything*.
   d. Spacing: Double space all lines, all pages, everything, *all the time*.
   e. Indentation: ½ inch for the first line of body text paragraphs. Use the auto-indent feature of your word processing program. Do not use hard tabs for paragraph indentation.
   f. Numbering: Number all pages consecutively with the number in the upper right corner.
   g. Notes: *Do not* use the embedded footnote feature of Microsoft Word. Place all notes at the end of the work.

h. Headers: *Do not* insert headers or footers (except for page number) or any graphics (including lines, arrows, borders, and shading).

3. Combine all chapters of your book into a single electronic file.

4. Insert a section break (next page) between chapters and other major elements.

5. You may use up to three levels of subheads, A-, B-, and C-level.

CHAPTER TITLE

(CENTERED, BOLD, SMALL CAPS)

A LEVEL SUB HEAD

(CENTERED, BOLD, SMALL CAPS)

B LEVEL HEAD (FLUSH LEFT, BOLD)

C Level Head. If you use C level heads, run them into the paragraph, use italics and punctuation.

II. DOCUMENTATION

A. DOCUMENTATION REQUIREMENTS

1. You may use either the standard method of documentation or the author-date method (see below). The standard method is preferred for all texts except those written on subjects in the humanities.

2. You are required to submit documentation with your manuscript to validate the accuracy of all cited material,

including quotations, statistics, research findings, or references to another work.

3. Submit the following for each use of quoted material:
   a. Photocopy of the full quotation or reprinted item *from its original source* (photocopy the full page, including the page numbers).
   b. Photocopy of title and author of source (usually the title page).
   c. Photocopy of the publisher, the copyright holder, and the copyright year (usually the imprint page).
   d. If permission is necessary for the use of quoted material, the original completed permission form or the copyright holder's completed response (letter, contract).

   e. Proof of payment (photocopy of canceled check) of any fees required by the copyright holder for use of quoted material.
   f. Documentation as listed above for any internal quotations.
   g. Photocopy of any footnotes or endnotes referenced in quoted material.

4. Submit the following for each use of factual information:
   a. Photocopy of the supporting documentation that verifies the factual information (photocopy the full page, including the page numbers).
   b. Photocopy of title and author of source (usually the title page).
   c. Photocopy of the publisher, the copyright holder, and the copyright year (usually the imprint page).

5. Submit the following for each use of a person's name or story:
   a. Written permission from the person to use his or her name or story.
   b. Written permission from a parent or legal guardian if the name or story is that of a minor.

B. Standard Method

1. Do not use the embedded notes feature in your word processing program. Mark the point where the note occurs like this: (footnote 1). Include notes at the end of the document or in a separate document.

2. In the notes section, mark the notes for each chapter with a subhead. Restart numbering for each chapter.

3. Double space and indent notes, just like text.

C. Author-Date Method

1. This style of documentation is often used when writing on the humanities. It includes a complete list of sources as well as abbreviated parenthetical citations in the text.

2. On the sources page, alphabetize works cited according to author's last name.

3. Double space and indent notes, just like text.

III. PERMISSIONS

A. USING COPYRIGHTED MATERIALS

1. The author is responsible for providing documentation for all quoted material and for obtaining permission from copyright holders and paying fees to use any quoted or reprinted material in your work.

2. Approved documentation for each permission is *required when you submit the manuscript.* Securing permission to use copyrighted material is a process that can take months. It is important to start the process immediately.

3. You may use the attached forms for each permission request. Be aware, however, that copyright holders may respond with their own contracts. In such cases, pay close attention to any restrictions and discuss them with your editor.

4. When is permission necessary?
   Copyright law covers all "works of authorship"—the written word, prayers, music, cartoons, illustrations, photographs, film, charts, diagrams—in any form (print, electronic, visual, and so forth). Permission from copyright holders is required to use material (beyond the fair use guidelines) from copyrighted sources.

   Permission is granted by copyright holders for a *specific excerpt* (phrase, sentence, paragraph, and so forth) or item that you indicate, not as a blanket permission to use anything from the source. If you plan to use multiple quotations or other items from one source, you must obtain permission for each quotation/item. One letter will suffice, but you must cite in its entirety each quotation or item you plan to use.

79

You must seek permission if the material quoted is a complete copyrighted work, such as prayers, charts, graphs, illustrations, etc.

Unpublished material (papers, handouts, letters, etc.): These are protected by copyright, and you must seek permission.

In your work, quotations must be cited exactly as they appear in the source, including punctuation. Specific permission from the copyright holder is required to adapt *any* wording or structure. This includes making language gender inclusive.

5. How much material can be quoted without obtaining permission? Copyright law allows for the "fair use" of copyrighted material. We abide by the following fair use guidelines.

   a. Poetry (including song lyrics): You may use one line under fair use, but must request permission for two or more lines.

   b. Prose selections: You may use up to 300 words from one source. This means 300 words total in the manuscript, not just in one passage. You must request permission for over 300 words.

   c. Magazine or newspaper articles: You may use excerpts of up to 200 words or 20 percent of the whole, but you must request permission for over that amount.

Note: If "special use" is made of prose or poetry, that is—using it as a chapter opening, on a separate page, or if it is being used in an anthology, you must request permission for two or more lines of poetry and for prose excerpts of fifty or more words.

6. What is public domain?

Material published before 1923 is in the public domain,

which means that the copyright has expired. Note, however, that in the United States this applies only to works first published in the United States. The copyright term may vary for the same work in different countries.

You can use or adapt material in the public domain without getting permission. However, you must still give us complete source copy for documentation and credit purposes.

Be sure that the item you are using was actually *published* before 1923. Material written before that date but not published until later may still be copyrighted.

Adaptations, arrangements, or translations of public domain material may have been created later and may still be copyrighted.

7. What about quoting from out-of-print resources?
Out of print does not mean that the copyright has expired. An out-of-print resource is no longer being printed and made available by the publisher, but the copyright to the resource is still in effect. The same copyright laws and permission guidelines apply to resources that are out of print as to resources that are in print.

8. What about quoting from the Bible?
Most Bible publishers allow quotations and a generous number of verses. Consult guidelines printed in the works cited or see *The Christian Writer's Manual of Style.* If you exceed the free permission stated by the publisher, you are responsible for securing permission from the copyright holder and supplying documentation, as with any other source.

9. What about quoting from another resource that I wrote?
If you are the author of published books/articles and wish to quote from your own material beyond the fair use

guidelines, you must obtain permission from the publisher or copyright holder of your books or articles.

10. What about quoting from the Internet?
    Material from the Internet is often under copyright protection, although that may not be clearly indicated. Furthermore, Internet material often contains errors. If you submit material from an Internet source, you may be asked to provide a print source for documentation.

11. What if the material I'm quoting contains internal quotations from other sources?
    If a quotation you are using includes an internal quotation from a different source, you must supply documentation for the internal quotation as well as for your main quotation. This includes a copy of the internal quotation from its original source. If the internal quotation is copyrighted, it may require separate permission from its copyright holder.

12. May I use other people's ideas?
    When you *interpret* another person's ideas and apply them to your subject, you must use your own thoughts and write in your own words. Merely changing a few words of the original source is not acceptable. Interpreting another person's ideas does not require permission or credit.

    When you *discuss* another person's ideas without quoting, you must name the person or original source. This type of use does not require permission but does require credit.

    When you retell a story, write a new arrangement of a song, translate to another language, or otherwise *adapt* a creative work, you are making a derivative of the work.

Even if you use your own words, you must get the copyright holder's permission to adapt the work. This type of use requires both permission and credit.

13. Do I need permission to use people's names or stories?
Yes, you need permission. From both an ethical and a legal perspective, it is important that you get permission to use individuals' names or stories in our resources.

It is imperative that information given about people is correct, particularly in stories or examples that might cause embarrassment or difficulties for the person mentioned. A better option may be to use a generic name and change enough details so that the person cannot be identified.

If you use the name or story of a minor (under age 18), you must obtain written permission from a parent or legal guardian. Even this will not bind the minor after the age of majority and may not protect us from a complaint by the minor after he or she reaches the age of majority, so carefully weigh the necessity of using a minor's name or story.

14. How do you document factual information?
Factual information included in the manuscript (proper names, historic dates, statistics, etc. beyond what could be easily verified in a standard dictionary or Bible dictionary) must be accompanied by supporting documentation.

B. How to seek permission

If you have selected material from a copyrighted source or are using a person's story or name in your manuscript, please follow these instructions:

1. Fill out the attached permission request form, identifying the material quoted and giving your own address for the return. Please type or print clearly.

2. Attach a copy of the text you wish to reprint— usually the page of your manuscript on which the quotation appears. Circle or underline the quoted lines. (Include a self-addressed, stamped envelope. This may expedite what can be a lengthy process.)

3. Make copies of all requests and material that you send to copyright holders for your files.

4. When you receive a response from the copyright holder, please note, as per your contract, that you are responsible for the payment of any fees requested by the copyright holder. If the fees seem prohibitively high, you may want to consider deleting the excerpt or replacing it.

5. Once you have received written permission from the copyright holder and have made any required payment, submit the original form, all attached manuscript pages, and any contracts (including a copy of your check to the copyright holder if a permission fee was required) with your manuscript.

IV. Submitting Your Manuscript

1. Combine all parts of your book (except for any graphics) into a single electronic file.

2. Place section breaks (next page) between chapters or other major parts of the work.

3. Place any graphics in a separate electronic file (or submit in hard copy).

4. Submit all items by email in Microsoft Word or similar format.

5. Submit hard copy graphics by regular mail.

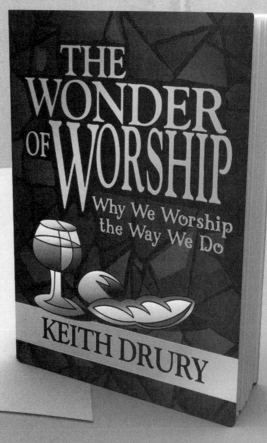

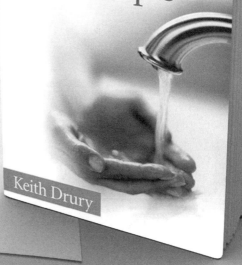